CONTENTS

INTRODUCTION

IN THE preface to Saunders Lewis's collected poems, Professor R. Geraint Gruffydd noted his belief that future selections of 'the poems that will continue to be part of the literary heritage of the Welsh during the generations and the centuries to come' would include a very high proportion of the contents of that volume. That is certainly the case with the present book, a selection and translation undertaken to commemorate the centenary year of the poet's birth.

For Saunders Lewis (1893–1984) was essentially a poet. How this informed his political vision and actions is matter for his biographers; how it grounded his literary criticism may be left to the literary historians. What is relevant here is that in publishing his dramatic masterpiece under the title of *Siwan a Cherddi Eraill* (Siwan and Other Poems), Saunders Lewis was not simply stating that the play was in verse – he was emphasizing that his imaginative writings all had the same source, in what Professor Gruffydd calls 'the special consciousness' that expresses itself in verbal images and harmonies, through the characters-in-action of the plays and novels, through the self-in-meditation of the short poems.

Compared to the bulk of the plays, those poems constitute a very slim volume. But it does not follow that they should be read as minor work, occasional by-products of Wales's greatest man-of-letters. Indeed, they refuse to be read that way. The present selection makes it evident that Saunders Lewis achieved what I take to be the essential mark of a major 'lyric' poet – not so much the accomplishment of a certain quantity of good poems as the imaginatively satisfying creation of a version of himself, a 'person in the poems' whose thoughts and feelings we experience as moments in the multifaceted life of one human being, who is *there* for us from poem to poem, so that each poem is enlarged and enriched by its relation to the others. This, I believe, is what Saunders Lewis himself was pointing to when he wrote that 'integrity . . . is a quality achieved objectively in the poem through the poet's craftsmanship and critical control . . . the making of a poem changes, transforms the [personal] experience, frames it in a new context so that its truth is now the truth of the poem'.

The person in Saunders Lewis's poems responds to the natural world at times with simple joy, in the muted wonder of the late poem 'May in the Garden' as in the extravagant celebration of the earliest poem 'A Daisy in April'. He experiences it at another time

vii

mythically, in 'The Dance of the Apple Tree'; at other times sacramentally, in 'The Pine' and 'Ascension Thursday', poems in which he is able for the moment to find in the natural world emblems of his Christian faith. In 'June Moon', however, he has a shockingly different experience of nature as empty and meaningless. And in 'Lavernock', he has yet another kind of epiphany, one that resists any simplifying commentary.

When these poems are read in the context and chronological sequence of the other poems, we experience them as occurring at intervals, and forming one strand that intertwines with the two others which Professor Gruffydd designates 'the world of man' and 'the world of God'. In the former it is Wales that provides situations and occasions to which the speaker responds as a member of a *polis*. The topicality of many of these poems has meant a subsequent loss of impact and appeal – they have not, in themselves, outlived their occasions, and I have excluded some of them in making my selection. But I have included others since they do contribute to our sense of a person immediately engaged by events within his society, and of a poet practising vigorously the traditional modes of eulogy and satire to express the beliefs and values essential for a sound community.

Even the less durable of such poems provide a context for and are partially revivified by those that retain power, such as 'The Deluge 1939'. This is very much a poem of its historical moment, but it remains far more than a historical document in dramatizing the speaker's agonized, revolted, and enraged contemplation of the Depression and the coming of war. What has disturbed many readers since its first publication, the contempt for the 'frail rabble', belongs none the less to what the poet once called the 'spiritual unity' of poetry, 'the truth of a thing, a *res*'. While we may wish the speaker had felt more compassion here, as for the English refugees in 'Scene in a Café', we can still comprehend his outrage at the cultural dehumanization he is witnessing and respond to these feelings, uncomfortable and even unChristian as we may find them, as an integral part of the poem. (So, too, with what we are likely to find still more disturbing, the ethnic caricaturing that is part of the satirical approach in these poems.) Both of these poems in turn enrich our response to the moving meditation on 'Saint David's Last Sermon' and to 'Saint Michael's Summer 1941', in which the natural world provides still another epiphany in time of war. The magnificent 'Elegy for Sir John Edward Lloyd' is a kind of climax, a drawing together of the recurrent concerns of the political poems that precede it, and a placing of them in a perspective which, as Professor Gruffydd has stressed, sees Wales 'as part of Europe and part of total humanity'. The last poem Saunders Lewis published, 'A Word to the Welsh' in 1980, was in response to one episode in the campaign for a Welsh-language television channel – taken by itself, this has suffered the same fate as the earlier topical poems, but within this selection it can be seen as a final cry of anguished love, a final call for the awakening of the Welsh people, a final passionate declaration that Wales 'will not die without witnesses', however few.

It is the third strand, the experience of God, that as we move from poem to poem grounds and illuminates the other experiences. The speaker in 'To the Blessed Sacrament', as he expresses with warmth and wry wit his love for his anti-papist friends, does not entirely avoid the temptation that belief in the Real Presence holds for Roman Catholics (I write as one of them) – to condescend to one's Protestant neighbour while taking pride in one's 'election' to a particularly difficult article of faith. But it is the same speaker who celebrates the grace that enabled the Good Thief to see and know Jesus as God in the hour of the crucifixion; who in 'The Carpenter' narrates sympathetically Saint Joseph's crisis of faith; who meditates on Mary Magdalen's traumatic loss of the presence of Jesus as the purgatorial experience, the participation in Christ's passion, required by divine love. Christian faith offers no easy answers and no easy life for this speaker, nor is it easily sustained. In 'Return' he sees an ironic parallel between his younger self's experience of love and his present knowledge of despair. It is this speaker who in 'Et Homo Factus Est. Crucifixus . . .' sees killing as the primal urge of mankind and finds bleakly, desperately, the one link to God in the consecration of the Christmas Mass.

Saunders Lewis's poems form, in their range and depth, a whole that is greater than its parts. The three 'worlds', which I have followed Professor Gruffydd in distinguishing as the most useful general approach to the work, become as one reads through this selection the integrated experiences of one passionate, thoughtful, believing, questioning person in a single complex world. It was for this person that Saunders Lewis found a grimly witty, starkly courageous voice as he confronted the limits of knowledge and faith in what became, appropriately, his last major poem, 'Prayer at the End'.

Bruce Griffiths comments in his excellent monograph on Saunders Lewis (University of Wales Press, 1976) that the losses inevitable in translation are especially true for this poet's style, 'with its echoes not only of Eliot, of Apollinaire, Laforgue, Verhaeren, of Vergil, but also of the vocabulary of classical Welsh poetry'. So too with his eclectic use of verse-forms, which include *cywyddau* and *awdlau* (gaining for eulogy and elegy a harmonic richness from the Welsh strict metres which evokes the cultural tradition celebrated by these poems), English sonnets, a variety of rhyming stanzas, and full-breathed free verse. I hope none the less that these translations suggest something of his stylistic and metrical range, his technical mastery of his genre.

I am grateful to Professor R. Geraint Gruffydd, as Saunders Lewis's literary executor, for his permission to undertake this commemorative volume, and for his advice. The translations are based on the texts in his *Cerddi Saunders Lewis* (Gwasg Gregynog, 1986; revised edition, Gwasg Prifysgol Cymru, 1992), and I have followed his chronological ordering of the poems. I have drawn on his annotations, but have expanded on them considerably in providing my own section of notes.

As so often over the past twenty years, I am indebted to Emeritus Professor R. M. Jones of the University College of Wales, Aberystwyth, for his encouragement and suggestions.

Eleven of the translations were published in my *Twentieth Century Welsh Poems* (Gomer, 1982). These have been revised, as have the translations of 'Prayer at the End' and 'Chance Child' published respectively in *Llais Llyfrau* and *Planet*. The introduction has been adapted from my review of *Cerddi Saunders Lewis* for *Planet* in 1987.

A DAISY IN APRIL

Yesterday I saw a daisy,
like a mirror of daybreak's beauty;
the day before, I trod heedless,
and yesterday, saw. How well I know
spring's passionate vigour and zest
creating its crystal shilling,
the force of the moorland's art,
ruby and gem in the marsh.
The field where an April cuckoo
sang has turned Milky Way;
the firmament's topsy-turvy,
millions of heaven's suns
are underfoot, put in place
to gild the earth's pallid lawn;
Orion on the hill-breasts,
Arcturus and Sirius there,
butterflies' beads of fire,
like stars awake, seraphic,
on a blue resplendent sky.
Yesterday I saw a daisy.

TO THE BLESSED SACRAMENT

*(On a visit by a number of my anti-papist friends
to a Catholic church)*

These, who came to your house
And sat somewhat fearful and half-defiant
Without greeting the Host or genuflecting,
Oh Master of Hospitality, do not be vexed
By their discourtesy;
Since in your hall is nothing
But an altar, its flowers and candlesticks helter-skelter and jumbled
Like a full sideboard in a second-hand furniture shop,
And sorry laughable pictures of your Passion and your Cross,
And images in Brummagem plaster of Joseph and Mary
Standing like an Aunt Sally at the fair,
And Saint Theresa like a fashion photo in *Vogue*.

These who came beneath your roof
As to Madame Tussaud's chamber of horrors,
How could they comprehend your marvellous tender mischief?
Your solemn children
With their sober zeal not to make of you an idol,
Here amid the bric-a-brac of our bit of ritual,
Take, uncontemptuous Father,
Their sharp contempt as true worship.

Since who in his right mind,
Lacking a better candle,
(Oh Father of lights),
Would ever perceive you playing hide-and-seek with your land
In the form
Of wheat,
An insignificant scrap in all of the clutter?
No wonder the children will not kneel to their missing Lord.

But when the day comes
That they tread your heavens without contempt
And kneel wondering there to the form of your manhood,
We, your poor captives
Whom you punished here with the Faith's biting cord,
May we have a share with your children of their wonder.

THE PINE

Still, the lake of night in the valley,
In its windless trough;
Orion and the Dragon sleep on its leaden surface,
Slowly the moon rises and sleepily floats on its way.

See now its ascension's hour.
At once you flare before it, a lance your leap
From base to crest beneath its travail,
Shooting to the heart of the gloom like the Paschal Candle under
            its flame:
Hush, the night stands round you in the tranquil chancel
As heaven's host crosses the earth with its blessing.

SCENE IN A CAFÉ

From the flurry of the uniformed garrison
And their turmoil in Great Darkgate Street,
Amid the throng that was spilled from the market and the college
And the chapel vestries and the pubs,
Amid the motley horde,
The sad horde that had lost the goodness of intellect,
The living dead,
Amid the cheerless cackle and red claws of females,
Their brute lips like a wanton nightmare rending
The sleep of their gorilla faces,
Amid the horde in flight,
In flight from the death of the sky and the life of the bomb,
Amid the chatting skeletons, the strolling ashes,
We squeezed through the café doors
Concealing our vacant skulls behind our fig-leaves,
And snatched a table-corner from Babel's band,
And shouted above the bones and the tea things
To a maid near by.

How swift was the maid's service, –
She brought us oysters and Kosher vinegar and the burial rite on
    toast.
The rain fell like a parachute on the street,
But the civil guard of ash-bins
Stood like policemen in a file near their houses.
And an old hag went, a rope around her neck,
From bin to bin in the rain, and raised each lid,
And found them, every coffin, empty.
And at the bottom of the road,
In the presence of the ravenous ashes there in the café,
The ashes that had escaped from the bins,
Whitechapel's lard-bellied women, Golders Green Ethiopians,
On a handy lamp-post, the hag hanged herself, with her rope.
We saw her shanks turning in the rain,
And we knew by her white gloves with their smell of camphor
That she'd come from the old land.
She was buried non-denominationally by the BBC
On the imperial wave-length.

To Dr J. D. Jones, CH

(formerly of Bournemouth)

From your feather pulpit your tallow sermon
   Trickled down on the gluttons,
And the grease drippings of your unctuous English
   Were the gorgers' means of grace.

You return now to the poor-man's-land
   That's crushed beneath the bigshot's thumb,
With your sharp rebuke to a fragile nation
   To bow to the yoke and the rope.

GARTHEWIN

An Ode in Praise of Robert Wynne

Seats of manners, for long ages they have been
   Foreign acres in our land,
   Old mansions lacking the common people's
   Sweet Welsh language, and their laughter;

Lacking local poets' laughter and the wine of their flattery,
   Lacking beautiful praise in speech,
   Without a hearth in the province,
   Men without kin, foreign language;

Baron and foreigner lacking their home patch's discourse,
   Lacking its virtue and hope,
   The manor lacking the precious language
   Withered as a scarred oak;

Like an oak fallen prey to lightning
   Or the blight of wasting disease,
   In its cheerless winter
   Of no good to the land, unemployed.

Your work on the land, let us bless your acres,
Governing for your country your fathers' estate,
Opening to common people your house and its relics,
Giving the mansion a servant's dignity to perfect it.

A hearth for the nation, your dwelling-places;
Like Owain's Sycharth, honoured Garthewin;
Congenial peer to the Wales of ancient days;
Courteous, bountiful, the gleaming white fortress.

There, as before, there are poets round the tables,
Garthewin has not lacked beer for its tenants,
I have drunk its wine from the harvests
Of Oporto, Bordeaux, the South's pretty river-mouths.

Sweet the chants in the people's court
To Mary, Winifred, the prayers to David;
The luminous sequence of the generations,
The old land of wax candles' invisible choir,

They love the spot where the sacraments on high
Breathe over our fragile nation;
And gentler the gentry of Wales in their graves
For the return to office of a nobleman from their seats.

AGAINST PURGATORY

Death, when you come, don't kill me like a dog
    With gunshot or bomb-blast, swiftly, suddenly,
Or in my sleep, lest I slip into your claws
    With no shudder, no summons, no outcry, no alarm;
Don't delay till the winter of weariness comes
    When all zest and desire are unaroused,
And the sap of old passions dozes beneath my dryness
    Until a new world wakes in a new spring;
But like a sturdy woodsman choosing a tree
    Come to me; sing with your axe a solemn warning,
And strike – once, twice – until the flakes of bark
    Spurt, and the branches shake, and bend their loads;
Uproot me from the earth, before it comes to pass:
The furnace-work of the charcoal-burners over there.

TO THE GOOD THIEF

You did not see Him on the mount of the Transfiguration
    Or the night He walked the sea;
You never saw corpses colour when bier and grave
    Felt the force of His cry.

It was in the hour of His flaying and His filth you saw Him,
    Under whip, under thorns,
And nailed, a sack of bones, outside the city,
    On a stick, like a scarecrow.

You did not hear the parables shaped like a Parthenon of language,
    Or His tone in talking of His Father,
Neither did you hear the secrets of the upper room,
    Or the prayer before Cedron and betrayal.

It was in the revel of a crowd of sadists carousing on sorrow,
    And their shriek, howl, curse, and shout,
You heard the profound lament of the broken heart of their prey,
    'Why have You forsaken me?'

You, crucified on the right; on the left, your brother;
    Writhing like toads that were skinned,
Flea-ridden pilferers tossed as retainers to deride Him,
    Courtiers for a mock king in agony.

Oh master of courtesy and manners, who enlightened for you
    Your part in the savage charade?
'Lord, when you enter your kingdom, remember me,' –
    The kingdom conquered by dying.

Rex Judaeorum; you were the first to see the mocking
    Blasphemy as a living oracle,
You were first to believe in the Latin, Hebrew, and Greek,
    That a cross was God's throne.

Oh thief who stole Paradise from the nails of a stake,
    Leader of heaven's nobility,
Pray that it may be given us too, before the hour of our death,
    To see Him and know Him.

THE DELUGE 1939

I

The tramway climbs from Merthyr to Dowlais,
Snail's slime on a slag-heap;
Here, once, was Wales, and now
Ruins of cinemas and rain on sterile tips;
The pawnbrokers have shut their doors; pegging clerks
Are the princes of the prairie;
All flesh has corrupted its way on the face of the earth.

My own life the same, seconder of the resolutions
That pass from committee to committee to set the old land on its
            feet;
Were it not better to stand on the corner in Tonypandy
And look up the valley and down the valley
At the flotsam of men's shipwrecks on the mud of despair,
Men and tips standing idle, for slag-heap and man the same end.

Where once were eyes there is dust and we unaware of our dying,
Our mothers thoughtlessly buried us, giving us milk of Lethe,
We cannot bleed like the men who came before us,
And our hands, they would be like hands had they thumbs;
Should our feet be shattered by a fall, we merely creep to a clinic,
Doff cap for a wooden leg and insurance and a Mond pension;
We command no language or dialect, are unconscious of insult,
And the masterpiece we gave history is our land's MPs.

II

The dregs arose from the empty docks
Across the dry ropes and the rust of cranes,
Their proletarian flood-tide crept,
Greasily humble, to the chip-shops,
Loitered, blood about the feet of policemen,
And spread, a lake of siliconic spit,
Through the faceless valleys of the industry of the dole.

Rain spilled its persistent needles
On the soft palms of old colliery hands,
Hail spattered on the leather breasts
Of dried-up mothers and their shrivelled babies,
Cows' milk was turned to umbrella sticks
Where rickets crooked the legs of young girls;
Old age pensions were given to the boys of the dole.

Nevertheless the moon was keeping her phases
And Apollo was washing his hair in the dew,
As when the wise were seizing their day
Among the Sabine hills, centuries ago;
But Saturn, Jove, and the Babe's golden age,
In turn they perished; the sad desolation
Of chimney ashes and vain child-bearing
Has drowned the stars beneath the slime of the dole.

III

In the beginning, this was not how we saw it:
We supposed it was merely the redemptive ebb and flow, the thrifty
        unsettling
Our masters would bless as part of the economic law,
The new scientific order that had cast out the natural law
As Jove supplanted Saturn, a zenithless progress of being.
And we had faith in our masters: we placed on them priestly garb,
Tortoise-shell glasses and plus-fours for preaching,
For preaching the sanctity of the surplus of jobless and prices'
        flexible providence;
And one day in seven, lest a courteous custom be broken,
We would sacrifice an hour to the pretty charm of antiquity
And in our fathers' old Pantheons we'd sing a psalm.

Then, on Olympus, in Wall Street, nineteen hundred and twenty-
        nine,
At their infinitely scientific task of guiding the profits of fate,
The gods determined, their feet in the Aubusson carpet
And their Hebrew nostrils in the quarter's statistics,
That the day had come to lessen credit through the universe of
        gold.

They did not know, earth's latest deities,
They were loosing the world's last floodgates;
They did not see the men on the march,
The clenched fists and the menacing arms,
Rank after rank through the agonies of Vienna,
Munich's deaf frenzy of raving,
Or the dragging feet and feeble cheep of the procession
Of jobless sleepwalkers and their torpid torment.

But so it was: the woe of mothers wailing,
The sound of men like the sound of dogs whining,
And a myriad myriad hurling themselves without hope
To the starless ditch and the regardless rest.
The prudence of the nations' rulers, it failed,
Dragons' teeth were sown in the acres of Europe,
Bruening went away from their seething passions,
From the cacklings of Basel and its foul money-lenders,
The husks and the hulls of the horde of Geneva,
To his long silent fast and his exile.
And the fragile rabble, the half-penny *demos*,
Base progeny of the greyhounds and the football pool,
Filled its belly with filthy pictures
And with the rotten chaff of the press and the radio.

But the sky of Ebro's region blackened,
Blood became wine for our famished passions,
And paralysis froze the faulty will
Of Basel's and Geneva's impotent wretches.
We saw we'd been duped. A goblin's vile deception
Festering our end was the skill of our gods;
Toppled and ravished reason's masterpiece
And our peerless idol, unshackled man;
The masters of the planet's resplendent credo,
Man's faith in man, that was snuffed out:
We the blank-faced mighty – measurers
    Of the stars and the suns on high,
    Profitless was the journey,
    Futile all joy,
The deluge of despair is our black refuge.

And across the wave comes the sound of tanks mustering.

THE CARCASS

'Many ask, Welshmen among them, why it should be allowed to live.'
Article in Y *Llenor*, Summer 1941

The carcass of Wales is lying here, sorely abused,
  With not many to weep for her misfortune,
Her conqueror's wretched slave-girl – yesterday found
  To his fancy – today, a turd.

To lick her disgrace and muck her about underfoot
  They gather together, the shabby herd
Of magistrate swine, grunting above her blood,
  And the frenzied bitches of parliament.

What is the stench that's moving within her flesh?
  Tapeworms, a swarm of officials
Growing fat on the death of a poor motherland;

And on her forehead, see – a black toad
  Croaking before the day of judgement
A quaking summons to the shameless desecration.

SAINT DAVID'S LAST SERMON

Strange, the sermon that David preached
After mass, the Sunday before the first of March,
To the crowd who had come there to grieve for his dying:
'Brothers and sisters, be cheerful,
Keep the faith, and do the little things
You have seen and heard from me.
As for me, I will go the road our fathers went.
Fare you well,' David said,
'And never, henceforth, shall we see one another.'
Such is the sermon, according to Llan Ddewi Brefi's hermit,
More ample than in Rhygyfarch's Latin,
And perhaps it was the memory of devout country people
Who roamed Teifi's banks, like rosary beads
Slipping one by one through the fingers of the centuries,
Preserved the version the hermit transferred to his parchment.

There was never so imperial a sunset
As David's proceeding from the synod of Brefi
To his dying in the dawn and the vale of roses.
Just a week before, at the morning service,
The banns of his liberation had been published to him
By an angel in the choir; and by an angel
The word was spread through the churches of Wales and the
           churches
Of kindly Ireland. They came thronging to Tŷ Ddewi,
The saints of both islands celebrating the funeral of their saint;
The city was filled with tears and wailing
And lamenting: Oh that the earth would swallow us,
Oh that the sea would overwhelm the land, Oh that the mighty
Mountains would fall upon us.
And on the first of March
There came to the church tearful the church triumphant,
And the sun, and heaven's nine orders, with songs and perfume;
David went, wonder by wonder, to his God.

Such is the story according to Rhygyfarch
In the hour of his heavy-heartedness at Llanbadarn Fawr.
In the hour of the clergy's anxiety and the country's anguish,
David's ancient writings in his chest
With the old chronicle and the clerics' relics,
The remnant of the greatness that had been, and that had been
        precious,
In the troubled cloister, in the reminiscent cell.
Such, two centuries later, is the story
According to the anchorite who copied it near the hill
That was once the site of Brefi's synod and the saint's feet and the
        miracle.
But no miracle, no angel, were found in David's sermon
After mass, the Sunday before the first of March,
For the crowd who had come there to grieve for his dying,
No summoning of the cloister as witness to the glories;
But an urging to the lowly paths: Be cheerful
And keep the faith and do the little things
You have seen and heard from me.

It has been a fearsome thing to historians, the rule of David,
With the Egyptian whip of his abstinence and the heavy yoke,
Lord of the saints, great-grandson of Cunedda and the purple.
But his final words, the sermon that nested in the memory
Of those who prayed on Teifi's banks through centuries
Of terror, through war, beneath the frown of the vulture-like
        castles,
Through the ages when the grasshopper was a burden,
They were maidenly words, a nun's tenderness,
'The little way' of Theresa to the purification and the union,
And the way of the poor lass who saw Mary at Lourdes.

THE CHOICE

The final massacre was over. The world was made one.
No turmoil, not one revolt from now on,
But order like a railway where once there was blood,
Every knee bending tamely, tame every face.
The Dictator rose from his costly campaigning,
Five continents docile beneath his feet;
He could take delight in what had been accomplished,
And stroll calmly among his silent subjects.

And he came to a desolate hill, with a cross
And upon it one who was dying. The monarch laughed,
'If you are the Son of God, come down from your pain,
Let the world choose between us; save yourself.'
And under the iron nails the Sacrifice said,
'Here I w. l be till world and man are no more.'

The Carpenter

Grave, in his workshop's shadow,
The carpenter's look, from daybreak
    Till late afternoon;
He knew his hand was trembling
Now, from the painful gladness
Of the silent song that nested
    In his full heart.

When the hour of sunset came
She would come too, his betrothed,
    A pitcher in either hand,
She would come, the bright one, beloved,
From the fountain and through the gardens,
And stand for a brief moment
    There, on the threshold.

His heart's song could never ever
Say how immaculate
    The maiden Mary was;
Wells, deep and tranquil,
Mirrors to invisible
Stars, were her sweet eyes,
    Chaste virgin.

Radiant early primroses,
April dew on a violet,
    The modesty of her step;
Like heaven's banner blinding
The wanton eye, her walking;
All would be pure in gazing
    At the flawless maid.

He shut the lids of his eyes,
His waiting like a prayer;
    He knew her step;
He looked hard; between the pitchers,
Between his betrothed's two arms,
He saw across her loins
    A mother's shape.

Mary stood on the threshold,
'Joseph.' And he groaned,
  'Are you a virgin, you?'
Tenderly, steadily,
The living Christ in her loins,
The undefiled one answered,
  'I am a virgin.'

What sharp-stabbing doubts,
What salt hours of torment,
  Did he not know;
Wild armies of demons,
Stunned disappointment, sullen despair,
Were putting it in his heart
  To curse heaven's heir.

Night came upon his soul;
There was no prayer, no light,
  No star, no dawn;
Mutely, without a sigh,
He was swaying on his knees
Until the devils struck him
  Like a dead man to the ground.

And in his dream he heard
An angel say, 'Do not fear
  To take Mary as a wife;
The Son she has been given,
He comes from the Holy Ghost,
And through him has been promised
  The crushing of the Dragon's head.'

And sunlight was on the dew
When the carpenter went to his workshop,
  Silent, from his dream,
And he sawed a handsome board of cedar,
Planed it smooth and polished it,
And on the comely plank he drew
  The pattern of a cradle.

SAINT MICHAEL'S SUMMER 1941

There was no spring, and rare was a flash of sun
On the swallow's bright blue flitting beneath the bridge;
The grain was sprouting in the ear in August
Because of the moist, sultry summer:
Women, their ears clamped to a voice in a box,
And the post so slow from Egypt, from Singapore,
'There's dreadful killing in Russia, I should think,'
And the rain falling like worry day after day
On bowed necks that spoke their grief sooner than words;
That was the war in our village,
A blackness of thunder turning and turning
Around us and above, a wall drawing closer,
Roaring and massing and bearing its lightning;
And on the mantel, a voice in a box boasting,
And the postman drawing his story out door to door
And the familiar names, Cardiff . . . Swansea . . . The South,
Meaningless terror lingering; foreign faces, tongues;
No one is saying what he thinks, no one
Is thinking; the voice in the box is boasting of
Our navy, *our* air force,
And we are reluctant to believe that our is our,
And go like those under a spell to the yard and the field
Where our hands feel the comfort of things that are old and certain
In the August rain.

But the wind turned. Mist came in the early morning
And was dispersed by a regal and leisurely sun,
A stretched-out afternoon and a sunset under banners,
And the Plough like a belt on the waist of night;
The gambo was loaded in the cornfields,
And in the orchard, among green apples,
Dewdrops sparkled on the tranquil gossamer;
Michael raised for us a hill of healing,
A glade of heat and balm at September's end,
Before the winter, before the testing, before the night's
                    thrumming,
Before raising anchor and sailing like Ulysses
Beyond the last headland in the land of the living:

'Brothers, do not begrudge this experience either
To the moment, Oh so brief, that still remains
For us to see and to taste the fair and the foul of the world,'
And he turned his ship toward the unknown stars . . .
And Dante saw him with Diomed.

Michael, who loves the hills, pray for Wales,
Michael, friend of the afflicted, remember us.

THE DANCE OF THE APPLE TREE

The apple tree's dance beneath its blossoms,
Bride of sweet-scented May;
Lamp singing an opal carol,
Pink-flushed in a flame of crystal
Like snow; sweet conjuror
Who lures the swarms of bees with their golden commotion
To crown its hair with their music,
Pouring out between the cambric white and the emerald.

Enchanting, September's apple tree;
I see the daughters of Atlas beneath it
Lifting their hands, Eritheia,
Hesper, Aegle, Arethusa,
Toward the green lanterns, round
As moons or the hidden breasts of the bright maidens
Who tend the winterless garden;
A dance of goddesses underneath apples, that's what I see.

21

T. GWYNN JONES

I sing, I celebrate the noble muse
    Of the Isle of Britain's High Bard;
  A civilized nation loves, well-wrought language,
  To glorify the hero I praise.

Hero of language, its translator, fashioner in verse
    Of splendid utterance,
  The brother of Cynddelw Brydydd shapes song
  Possessing the power of Gwyn ap Nudd.

In the day of maimed, mongrel versifying
    Came the master-poets' gift,
  Fair star of thousands who perceive it,
  Radiant sign of the zodiac, sublime grace.

Grace the age's shifting fortunes cannot shatter;
    Stronger than brass; it will not be
  Reduced to rubble, not by the irreversible
  Turn of the wheel or narrow-minded dispraise.

MARY MAGDALEN

'Do not touch me'

No one can know about women. There are those,
Like her, for whom their pain is a locked grave;
Their pain is buried within them, there is no fleeing
From it, or being delivered. There is no ebb
Or flow to their pain, a dead sea with no
Movement upon its deep. Who – is there anyone –
Will sometime roll the stone from the grave?

See the dust trailing limply along the path:
No, let her be, Mary is going to her peace,
Deep calling unto deep, grave to grave,
Corpse drawn to corpse in the cheerless dawn:
Three days she has been in a grave, in a world ended
In the afternoon outcry, the word Finished,
The cry that bled her heart like the point of a sword.

Finished, Finished. Mary fell from the hill
To the void of the final Pasch, to the pit of a world
That was merely a grave, its breath in a silent grave,
Mary fell to the stunned death of perdition,
A world without a living Christ, creation's dread Sabbath,
The pit of the hundred thousand centuries and their obliteration,
Mary lay in quivering creation's grave,

In the trough of the night of the senses, in the smoke's cauldron;
The rich hair that had dried his feet turned white,
All memory's flowers faded save the shower of blood;
Cloud upon cloud enveloped her, their stench
A burning coal in her gullet, and ravaged her sight
Till God was snuffed out by their piercing terror,
In the dying together, the burial together, disgraced.

See her, Christ's Niobe, dragging to the hillside
The rock of her pain behind her from the leaden Pasch
Through the dark dawn, the cold dew, the heavy dust,
To the place with a stone heavier than her broken heart;
Clumsily the stumbling feet make their way across thorns,
Troublesome tears doubling the mist before her,
Her hands stretching toward him in naked yearning.

One luxury is left to her under the heavens,
One farewell caress, memorial tenderness, one
Final carnality, sad and consoling, sweet,
The chance to weep once more, clasping his legs,
To anoint the feet and wash the savage wounds,
To kiss the ankles and dry them once more with her hair,
The chance to touch You, Rabboni, Oh Son of Man.

We have pity for her. He had no pity.
Surpassing pity is the pure, blazing love
That tempers the saints' iron by blow after blow,
That scourges the flesh to its fort in the soul, and its home
In the heavenly spirit, and its burrow in the most holy,
That burns and slashes and tears till the final skirmish,
Till it strips and embraces its prey with its claw of steel.

She little knew, six days before the Pasch,
Pouring the moist precious nard upon him, all of it,
That truly 'she kept this for my burial';
She did not imagine, so precious his praise for her task,
That she would never, never more touch his feet or his hands;
Thomas could place his hand in his side; but she, despite her
    weeping,
Only in the pitiful form of Bread would the broken flesh now come
    to her.

There she is in the garden at the crack of dawn;
She presses her eyes toward the cave; she runs,
Runs to her remnant of paradise. Ah, does she believe,
Does she believe her eyes? The stone on the ground,
And the grave empty, the grave silent and bare;
The first lark rising above the bare hill,
And the nest of her heart empty and bereft.

As monotoned as a dove, her lament,
Like Orpheus mourning for Eurydice
She stands among the roses crying insatiably
'They have taken my Lord, have taken him,'
To disciple and to angel the same outcry
'And I do not know where they have laid him,'
And to the gardener the same raving.

She was stunned. She was shattered. She sank herself in her grief.
The mind reels and reason goes astray, unless
One comes who will snatch her out of the flesh to crown her –
Sudden as an eagle from the Alps stooping to its prey –
With the love that moves the stars, the strength that is a Word
To raise and give life: 'and He said to her, Mary,
And she turned and said to Him, Rabboni.'

ODE TO HIS GRACE, THE ARCHBISHOP
OF CARDIFF

The singing in times past for the son of Sant and Non,
    You, gentle joyous father,
In a night of scorn, in an age of deceit,
An age that spits on the bruises of its Pope,

You, our day's David, will not hear; alas for the virtue
    And the Welsh tongue of Christian poets;
In the anguish of the war against unbelief
It is pain to bear the crown of Cardiff.

The day of the odes of the Faith has fled, Teilo's land
    Will revere no Archbishop's robes;
God in bread, ha-ha, ho!
After Freud, the radio set,

What need of the Lord's Mass? The race is nothing but
    Cinema-worshippers flocking
From film to film, till it stops,
The cheering-up of life, at a single stroke,

In the beneficent civil night,
    Its family catholic,
The tribe growing quiet like a fair
At the clang of a bell, strong servant's harsh summons;
But a soul, from the dreadful disintegrating,
From the vale of phantoms will awake
Naked, belatedly sane, from the great deforming
    To a tomorrowless hour

Of silent fervent clinging to the hidden, wounded
    Calvaries of Wales
And the sweet strength of the memorial offering,
In times past, of the infinite intercession;
There they will be valued, your ecclesiastical
Sacrifice, Jesus' chalice,
The unity of Christ's mediation, in heaven
    And beneath the sky;

And you will give them a door and an altar, bringing
   Goodness to Wales,
Under the throes of the stop-tap's chatter and trample, the
   murmur
Of the waltz's clamour, the jeering and the roaring,
Bringing Heaven's wealth to be hidden
And placing the Lamb of God in his house,
Bearing Patrick's Breastplate to prevent an ancient church's decay,
   The grace of Ann's daughter to purify it.

EMMAUS

No one will happen on it now;
its history but a single hour;
rock and path, trafficless
Emmaus is utterly lost.

But there abides, in its chronicle of events,
Christendom's Easter Sunday,
the generous discourse and the gracious invitation,
the consecration of Emmaus' bread.

What spectre in the distance there
is burrowing in the sand, at a late star-lit hour,
for a town near Jerusalem and its door?
For a road to Emmaus?

Phantom of Arab or Rabbi?
Ah, grief upon grief! Is it I
awaiting the dawn of the one brief hour
of Emmaus, that is no more?

MABON

Your life has lasted two quarters of a century, and Oh
The prison and the lanternless cell beneath the flow
Of youth's cataracting river of blood, and the wounds
Its gushes scarred upon you before the opening of the door.

Then Arthur arrived to save you, your Lord Arthur,
And snatch you into his battle, a knave to trade wounds with
            knaves
And savour the fellowship of his Table, and fling you to the
            beehives
Of the enemy gaol and the eunuch-hood of unprovisioned sand.

Your flesh will not see a third quarter-century;
The third prison has the shape of its shadow upon you
To fine you to the last farthing before you flee from its fate.

At this gaol's alarum, it will fall silent, the bewailing
Of wound, bar, lock, betrayal, till the doomed wretch at the last
            remembers
Arthur has gone before him, and his elegy turns to a *Te Deum*.

ARIANRHOD'S FORTRESS

(Owain's soliloquy before meeting the Abbot)

I saw the night close its wing over the moorland,
Over scant flimsy cottages, fallow land, infrequent furrow,
And the stars and Arianrhod's fortress came out, profound
      miracle,
To spatter the firmament's feathers with their thousand peacock
      eyes.

I spread the wing of my dream over you, my country;
I would have raised for you – Oh, if you'd wished it – a sweet
      fortress;
But one with the falling star, flung from amid the stars
To stain the gloom with its dawn that soon died, such is my state.

I read how, long ago, Aeneas went
Through the cavern with the Sybil, and to the land
Of Dis and the shades, like a man wayfaring
In a wood by night beneath the inconstant moon,
And there in gentle dusk
Beyond the river and the Field of Wailing,
He saw Troy's ancient heroes, ancestors of Rome,
Deiphobus with his wounds, earth's daring men,

The sons of Antenor and of pale Adrastus;
And they guided him, and crowded close beside him,
Till he came to a crossroads, to a gate,
Where his face was washed, the golden bough presented,
And a dale opened and groves
Delightful under stars and a clear purple sky,
Where Dardanus and Ilus and the griefless dead
Were lying in green meadows at their ease.

So I, one evening, led by Bangor's ancient seer,
I went down to the river, dared the boat,
Left the shoals of today where there is no anchor
And crossed the water, like ashes in night's pit,
To the darkness of the caves
Where among the trees stern phantoms stared
Whispering dead hunters' faint dead cry
I could not hear; a mere shape on a den's walls.

Then light came, and a form like a smiling dawn,
Helmet and cuirass sparkling and a brazen eagle
And trees were felled, ponies in the tides of Menai,
Hills were paved and fortresses roped in a row:
Tu regere . . . populos,
I saw the image of Agricola standing
On a beach in Môn, he was murmuring Vergil's prophecies,
The brine on the toga's hem like a snowdrift at nightfall.

And after him I could see a man turning
Off the road to the forest, to clear a glade
And sow his wheat and set a table and cover it;
And in his bearing was a mystery. He made
Slowly the sign of the cross,
And recited words of remembrance over the bread,
And slowly lifted a cup toward the dawn,
Knelt and beat his breast, communed with pain.

I hesitated: 'I know, while Europe lasts, will last
The memory of these; they will not wholly die,
Builders of the empires of the Cross and the Eagle;
Their dream, that tied beneath a single toll,
One people on one rock,
Môn and Cyrenaica, was a ground of hope
For Dante and for Grotius, was a screen for plunder
By Frederick the Second and sombre Philip of Spain.

But here in the region of shades is a race
Condemned to the pain of Sisyphus in the world,
To push from age to age through a thousand years
A stone nation to Freedom's hill-crest, and when –
Oh bitter lineage of Cunedda –
The hill's summit is in sight, through treachery or violence
The rock is hurled to the valley and the effort fails,
And the Birds of the Pit laugh at their latest pangs;

Where are these?' And look, a baneful hall,
A bed in the centre, bishop, archdeacon,
Tonsured monks, the priors of Chester, Shrewsbury,
Anointing the dark eyes of a terrible warlord,
And he gazing from his old age
At a fjord in Scandinavia, Gothri's ships marauding,
The cave of Ardudwy, the gaol of Hu Fras, Bron yr Erw,
The trials of the saga of an age and its agony under the ointment.

And I saw a gallows on a lawn and audacious hands
Reaching toward it between bars of iron,
Till a ship came from Aber and silent oarsmen,
Torches on the tide and ashes on a monarch's hair
And a cross between hands on a shrine . . .
And there, a head upon a spear, and horses' hair
Dragging in Shrewsbury's dust behind their harness
The battered body of the feeblest last of his line.

And for a moment, like a lighthouse's shaft of flame
Across the night's deluge, flashed the clefts of the fort
That stands on a cliff at Harlech, the heir of the two houses
Of Wales wearing a crown, a dance for the heir;
Then near Glyn y Groes
A second Teiresias in the dawn of Berwyn gave
The verdict of fate's oracle, and there was an end:
His shade melted in the mist that covered him.

Like him who climbed the cliffs of the land of despair
I turned to my leader, 'Can your thought
Ascend the steep of time and see a hope?
Their language they will keep, will the prophecy hold true?
Will the last relic
Of Cunedda be kept by his sons' painful labour?'
But he, the lantern-bearer of lost centuries,
He was there no longer, neither his lamp nor his word.

ELEGY FOR THOMAS GWYNN JONES

Elegies' trade has ended,
praise in verse-craft is stilled;
pointless in this age of mine
fine clichés of by-gone ages.
For a tiger of language, tears?
The grandeur was a torch, a wonder.
Our sorry speech's ashes,
a damp hearth's poor obsequies,
turned to flame, a rare bright rose,
in his hands, without a flaw,
an ardent unsinking flame,
look at its form, and marvel –
Madog, Tir na n-Og, Gwlad Hud,
Enlli, fervent Gwernyfed,
Broseliawnd, miraculous grove,
Arthur's isle and the springtime;
there laughs on them, no sad cold,
the wondrous sun of pure genius,
blossoms no scythe will cut down,
diamond flowers with soul of flame.
Should a night of poverty blight
our language and speech be stripped
by bungling councils, by a mongrel
university's warmed-up mash,
your odes will stand, your fame's gems,
gifted poet, to reproach
putting out the flame, fickle nation,
no poor half breeds will rekindle.
Your *Manion* is the judgement on us,
your *Cerddi* your prayer from the dung
for the dawn of Anatiomaros,
for bringing night-bound Wales from the mist.

ASCENSION THURSDAY

What is up, on the slopes, this May morning?
Look at them, at the gold of the broom and the laburnum
The glowing surplice on the hawthorn's shoulders,
The alert emerald of the grass, and the tranquil calves;

See the chestnut-tree's candelabra alight,
The bushes genuflecting and the mute birch nun,
The cuckoo's two notes across the stream's bright hush
And the mist wraith curling from the meadows' censer:

Come out, people, from the council-houses before
The rabbits scatter, come with the weasel to see
The raising from the earth of a spotless host
And the Father kissing the Son in the white dew.

JUNE MOON

Last night, at midnight,
A moon was full in a firmament,
In a starless, mistless void,
In the nightless abyss.

Not a shadow quivered, no whistling of an owl
In the moon-struck desolation.
The world died.

Yearning, in a fairweather nightmare,
For the meaningless grave of the moon.

LAVERNOCK

Moor and sea, the song of a lark
rising through the wind's precincts,
and ourselves standing to listen
as we'd listen long ago.

What is there left, what riches,
after the trials of our journey?
Moor and sea, the song of a lark
falling from the wind's precincts.

OLD MAN

Dust on my books, and I close by the grate;
I wear spectacles only to see my plate.

Why need you fear poverty when you're nearing death's door?
Not poverty's my fear, but being seen to be poor.

What has the eighty-year-old stirred up?
A girl has gone by, a dance in her skirt and her step.

JOTTINGS — AUGUST 1953

1. THE WHITETHROAT

The quick little bird, the whitethroat,
   Under the scarlet bean-blossoms,
As it was hunting aphids
   It roused a butterfly;

Away they go, flitter-flutter,
   Zig-zag, like playing hide-and-seek;
Before reaching the apple tree
   White-beaked is the whitethroat.

2. VANESSA IO

Empress of butterflies
On a peony throne, outspread,
Its wings like the peacock's train
Or Cleopatra's fan — alive.

3. PEACHES

Summer's velvet on the tongue, and its fruit's savour
   A sweet shiver on the palate,
   Firm-fleshed green and purple pouch,
   August's blood has filled your hollow.

CAROL

On the ancient tree sprung from Adam's grave,
Jesse's black and knotted trunk,
Was grafted a branch from heaven, and today,
Oh hosanna, Oh hosanna,
See – here is God's own rose.

In the starless night, no moonlight,
The pit of winter, in the year's
Senility – behold, a Baby,
The Son of Mary, Oh Sibyl,
The king of heaven was born.

Let a robin sing in the snow,
Let Melchior sing to his camels,
Let Vergil sing with Buddha:
Son of Mary, Alleluia,
Eia Jesu, Alleluia,
Praise to his name, all praise.

RETURN

When young I loved. Love kills
A world of people at one stroke:
No one exists but my love.

Creation's myriad illuminations
Are put out in that instant.
No sun, no moon but my love.

Now I know what it means to despair.
Despair, despair, it demolishes every being
Utterly, with its knelling.

MAY IN THE GARDEN

I

Seeing a fledgling sparrow
Bathe the first time in water,
Its wings splashing the bubbles
Like lilac foam.

II

Wings came from the sea,
The swift comes from swimming,
Through fifty million years
Its wings and feathers were fashioned,
A live arrow piercing air
Below, aslant, then aloft
And sleeping at the sky's zenith
On its wing, beneath the stars, with the flock.

ET HOMO FACTUS EST. CRUCIFIXUS . . .

(Christmas 1971)

And was made man. He was crucified.
What other course, what other fate
Could there be for heaven's son?
To kill is the primal instinct of mankind,
It's the amoeba's itch;
The most impassioned songs of the myriads of prey
Have been carols of pain and cantos of peril
Since the hewing of stone axes
In the doors of the caves,
The millions of generations of grief
Of an insignificant planet
Lost in the limitless void of being.

And here in the pit of darkness
In the winter of the earth,
Our shattered race's history's utmost hell,
We light a candle because a son is born to us
And we lift him from his cradle –
The frail baby is heavy,
He bears the weight of all the aeons of sin –
But we lift him up and we kill him,
I, Caiaphas,
You, Teiresias,
And set him aloft,
An altar hewn
From the world's anguish
To one who is, without him, an unknown God.

CHANCE CHILD

Chance befuddles prophets
And Marx's golden age, and Teilhard de Chardin's, demands
        a diceless evolution.
One can't get things set for a revolution
Or catch the future in a computer's
Nets. Life doesn't climb
Step by step,
But gives a leap from the fishes' maw and has wings
Or gets up on two feet and has a hand.

The scientists today assert
There's a host of earths in the planets of the universe,
Their climates like that which nourished man.
They want to greet them, and fortify them.
But if man is an accident, a matter of luck, good or bad,
Perhaps there is only this
One in all the star-clusters,
Here a few hours,
The chance child in the eternal silence:
Is there no one, is there just one, will reach him a hand?

MAY 1972

Once more the orchard is caroling
Once more the purple of the lilac's like young Tutankhamûn
Once more an hour after daybreak the morning's fragrance
Rises from the dew
The new-born earth's an immaculate virgin
I feel its breathing
Put a fingernail beneath a primrose leaf
Listen to the mystery of the bees
And the blackbird awake on its nest
Taste once more for a moment
Paradise.

PRAYER AT THE END

It's an experience everyone has that nobody else will know.
Each on his own in his own way
Owns his own dying
Through the millions of years of the human race.
You can look at it, you can sometimes recognize the moment;
You cannot empathize with anyone at that moment
When the breathing and the person stop together.
And then? Nothing reaches out to the then but a prayer groping.
Such a sorry creature is man, such a baby his imagination:
'In my Father's house there are many mansions',
As poor as our own, just as much earth-bound,
His intuition too in the days when he emptied himself.
And only this way can we ourselves picture hope:
'He is seated on the right hand of God the Father almighty' –
A general hailed with jubilation through the city of Rome
After the hazardous enterprise in a Persia of creation
And crowned as Augustus, Co-Augustus with his Father –
How laughable, the supreme assertions of our faith.
And around us remain silence and the pit of annihilation
Into which our universe will soundlessly fall some night.
Our words cannot trace the borders of silence
Or say God with meaning.
One prayer remains for all, to go silently to the silent.

A WORD TO THE WELSH

You Welsh, my kinsfolk,
Who have nurtured dreams of luxury on a Welshwoman's milk
      and breast,
And have garnered memory and conscience and all the guilt of
      adolescence
And the power to judge good and evil
From father and mother's word-stock and the voices of church or
      chapel,
Since without those there is no Welsh,
Consider now and judge,
You Welsh-speaking Welsh:
The government of the realm is announcing your end
And that there'll be no Welsh-speaking Wales,
Murder has been the goal of the government
For six centuries,
And today it sees it achieved.
The killing the Conquest did not attempt,
That the treason of the Union could not bring about,
That the thousand years of poverty,
Lacking dignity, lacking learning, lacking manners,
Did not manage,
Today pleasure and the business of pleasure with its greed and its
      babble in every kitchen and parlour of our land,
Under government patronage,
Is destroying our families and their faith,
Is accomplishing our death.

Rape is a tyrant's deed, *summa iniuria*,
The attribute of an unjust goverment,
'Customary after arrogance, a long death' –
Unless a shock and a challenge come to the nation of Wales, and a
      sudden awakening,
And a declaration to the world
That there is blood in her veins,
And she will not die without witnesses,
Be they but three.

NOTES

I have given the Welsh title and the year of first publication for each poem on the basis of Professor Geraint Gruffydd's notes in *Cerddi Saunders Lewis*, but I have not considered it necessary to include the further bibliographical information to be found there.

1 A DAISY IN APRIL *Llygad y Dydd yn Ebrill*, 1928

2 TO THE BLESSED SACRAMENT *I'r Sagrafen Fendigaid*, 1936
Roman Catholics believe in the doctrine of transubstantiation, namely that the bread and wine consecrated at Mass become the body and blood of Jesus Christ. In a Catholic church, consecrated wafers are kept in a tabernacle, and it is therefore customary to genuflect on entering and leaving the church. On certain occasions the church will observe 'exposition of the Blessed Sacrament' by placing a large consecrated host in a monstrance on the altar.
   Brummagem: cheap and showy (the word comes from an old form of 'Birmingham').
   Saint Theresa: of Lisieux (1873–97).
   Vogue: a women's fashion magazine.
   Madame Tussaud's: the famous waxworks museum in London contains a section devoted to famous murderers.

3 THE PINE *Y Pîn*, 1939
   the Dragon: the constellation Draco.
   the Paschal Candle: in Roman Catholic liturgy, at the Easter Vigil all lights in the church are put out and a large candle is lit from new fire, a symbol of 'the light of Christ', to celebrate the Resurrection.
   host: the wafer elevated by the priest at the consecration of the Mass.

4 SCENE IN A CAFÉ *Golygfa mewn Café*, 1940
The setting is Aberystwyth, the mid-Wales seaside resort and university town where evacuees from London and other English cities were lodged during World War II.

5 TO DR J.D. JONES, CH *I'r Dr J.D. Jones, CH*, 1940
The Reverend J. D. Jones, Companion of Honour, retired from Bournemouth to Llandderfel, and published his autobiography, *Three Score Years and Ten*, in 1940.

6   GARTHEWIN   *Garthewin,* 1941
Garthewin was a mansion in the parish of Llanfair Talhaearn, owned by R. O. F. Wynne. Some of Saunders Lewis's plays were first produced in the little theatre there.

Owain's Sycharth: Owain Glyndŵr's great fourteenth-century manor, celebrated in a famous poem by Iolo Goch. For a translation, see my *Medieval Welsh Lyrics* (Macmillan, 1965). Saunders Lewis's poem is in this tradition of praise for a generous nobleman, which has English parallels in such poems as Ben Jonson's 'To Penshurst'.

Oporto, Bordeaux: port comes from the former, in Portugal; claret from the latter, in France.

Winifred: a seventh-century Welsh saint, said to have spent her final years in Gwytherin, a village some eight miles from Garthewin.

8   AGAINST PURGATORY   *Rhag y Purdan,* 1941
According to Roman Catholic teaching, a person who makes a perfect act of contrition before the moment of death will enter heaven without having to undergo the purifying sufferings of Purgatory.

9   TO THE GOOD THIEF   *I'r Lleidr Da,* 1941
The poem is based on Saint Luke's Gospel, xxiii, 39–43.

10   THE DELUGE 1939   *Y Dilyw 1939,* 1942
The Oxford Companion to the Literature of Wales says of the Depression of the 1930s: 'In Wales there was a decline in the metallurgical and coal industries, as well as a virtual shut-down of the busy export ports along the southern coast. The numbers employed in coalmining alone fell from 270,000 in 1920 to 128,000 by 1939. The population of Wales was drained away to the new industrial areas of England with a total decline ... of nearly half a million persons. The standard of living fell, nutritional deficiencies marred the health of more than one generation, and a culture of unemployment settled on south Wales, a region of which the rate of long-term, mass unemployment exceeded that for any other part of Britain.'

Professor Gruffydd notes of Saunders Lewis's poem that after the first section's treatment of the Depression in south Wales, 'in the second section the picture is enriched with elements of the mythology of the ancient world (and the

Christian interpretation of it). The same mythology is used ironically for the third section, which traces the effects of the failure of the industrial world's financial system (symbolized by Wall Street in New York and Basel and Geneva in Switzerland) from 1929 on'.

pegging clerks: clerks at the labour exchange.

All flesh: the line echoes Genesis vi, 12.

Mond pension: Sir Alfred Mond, founder-chairman of Imperial Chemical Industries, led a group of twenty major employers in an effort to join with union leaders in reorganizing industry and increasing workers' benefits, beginning in 1928.

Lethe: in Graeco-Roman myth, the river of forgetfulness in Hades, the underworld.

Sabine hills: where the Roman poet Horace had his small farm-estate and wrote poems commending moderation in all things and the wisdom of *carpe diem,* seizing the day, enjoying the present moment.

Saturn: in Graeco-Roman myth, the god Saturn was overthrown by his son Jove (Jupiter).

the Babe's golden age: Vergil's fourth eclogue (*c.* 40 BC) celebrated the birth of a child (whose identity is still uncertain) as inaugurating a new age of gold. Medieval Christians interpreted the poem as a prophecy of the birth of Jesus.

Bruening: Heinrich Bruening (1885–1970) was the last democratic chancellor of Germany before Adolf Hitler came to power.

Ebro: a river in Spain, site in 1938 of the defeat of the Spanish government's army by the forces of General Francisco Franco, who became dictator.

Dragon's teeth: in the Greek myth of Cadmos, the hero sowed the teeth of the dragon he had slain and armed men sprang from the earth.

demos: the common people, a Greek word that is the root of 'democracy' but in the pejorative sense of 'mob rule'.

13   THE CARCASS   Y Gelain, 1942

The quotation is from an article by D. Emrys Evans, 'The War and the Choice', published in *Y Llenor* (Summer, 1941), the dominant Welsh-language literary magazine 1922–55.

14 SAINT DAVID'S LAST SERMON *Pregeth Olaf Dewi Sant,* 1942

Rhygyfarch, a member of the cloistered community at Llanbadarn Fawr, wrote a Life of St David about 1094, as part of a campaign to defend the independence of the bishopric of St David's. Rhygyfarch's father was Sulien, bishop of St David's. At about the same time he wrote a lamentation deploring the Norman attacks on Ceredigion.

According to Rhygyfarch, David, who had lived five centuries earlier, was a grandson of Ceredig, king of Ceredigion, one of the eight sons of the legendary Cunedda. David established his chief monastic community at Glyn Rhosyn, the Vale of Roses, now known as Tyddewi, St Davids. His rule for the monastery was notably ascetic: only water could be drunk, and the land was tilled by hauling the plough oneself. Near the end of his life, when David spoke at the synod in what is now Llanddewibrefi, it was said that the ground rose beneath his feet so that the crowd could see and hear him.

A later life of David is contained in *The Book of the Anchorite,* written in Welsh by a fourteenth-century hermit.

Egyptian whip: Christian monasticism originated in Egypt.

Theresa: Saint Theresa of Lisieux (1873–97) was a Carmelite nun whose 'little way' consisted of the faithful and prayerful performance of one's daily obligations.

the poor lass: Saint Bernadette (1844–79).

16 THE CHOICE   Y *Dewis,* 1942

17 THE CARPENTER   Y *Saer,* 1942

The basis for the poem is Saint Matthew's Gospel, i, 18–25.

19 SAINT MICHAEL'S SUMMER 1941   *Haf Bach Mihangel 1941,* 1942

Haf bach Mihangel, the little summer of Saint Michael, is the Welsh term for 'Indian summer', the last warm spell before the onset of winter. Saint Michael's feast-day is 29 September.

The summer of 1941 was an especially difficult one for the Allies in World War II. Their armies were under siege in North Africa; there was anxiety about Japan's intentions in the Far East (Pearl Harbor would be attacked on 7 December); Germany invaded Russia on 22 June and succeeded in advancing rapidly with great loss of Russian lives; the Luftwaffe was conducting night bombing raids on British cities, including Cardiff and Swansea.

the Plough : the constellation *Ursa Major.*

Ulysses: in Dante's *Inferno,* Canto xxvi, the ancient Greek hero Ulysses, imprisoned in a single flame with Diomed, tells of his final voyage.

21 THE DANCE OF THE APPLE TREE   *Dawns yr Afallen,* 1943

the daughters of Atlas: in Greek myth, the eleventh labour of Hercules was to fetch golden apples from the garden of the Hesperides, which was tended by the daughters of the giant Atlas.

22 T. GWYNN JONES   *T. Gwynn Jones,* 1944

Thomas Gwynn Jones (1871–1949), a major poet and translator of European literature into Welsh, was a leader in the Welsh literary revival of the earlier twentieth century. He is particularly noted for large-scale poems, using Celtic myths with modern implications, in an elevated style based on the diction and strict metres of medieval Welsh poetry.

Cynddelw: Cynddelw Brydydd Mawr (Cynddelw the Great Poet) was the foremost court poet of Wales during the later twelfth century.

Gwyn ap Nudd: ruler of the fairy world in Welsh folklore.

23 MARY MAGDALEN   *Mair Fadlen,* 1944

The poem is based on Saint John's Gospel, xx. The quotation at the beginning is from verse 17.

Niobe: in Greek myth, a queen punished for her maternal pride by the loss of all her children.

Orpheus: in Greek myth, the supreme poet-musician who descended into the underworld after the death of his wife Eurydice, won her release from Hades by his power of song, but lost her again when he disobeyed the command not to look back at her during the return to the upper world.

the love that moves the stars: the final line of Dante's *Paradiso* is *l'amor che move il sole e l'altre stelle,* 'the love that moves the sun and the other stars'.

26 ODE TO HIS GRACE, THE ARCHBISHOP OF CARDIFF *Awdl i'w Ras, Archesgob Caerdydd,* 1946

The poem is addressed to Michael Joseph McGrath (1882–1961), Bishop of Menevia 1935–40 and Archbishop of Cardiff 1940–61.

Sant and Non: the parents of Saint David.

Teilo's land: the territory of the sixth-century Saint Teilo corresponds by and large to the Archbishopric of Cardiff.

Patrick's Breastplate: a traditional Irish prayer attributed to Saint Patrick, which asks that Christ be within one's mind and heart in every action at every moment of the day.

Ann's daughter: the Virgin Mary.

28 EMMAUS *Emmaws,* 1946
The poem refers to Saint Luke's Gospel, xxiv, 13–35.

29 MABON *Mabon,* 1946
In the medieval Welsh tale of *Culhwch and Olwen,* Mabon son of Modron, who had been stolen from his mother when three days old, was found imprisoned in Gloucester and rescued by King Arthur, and subsequently took part in the hunting of the great boar Twrch Trwyth. Mabon is also mentioned as one of Arthur's men in a poem in *The Black Book of Carmarthen.*

Whatever Saunders Lewis may have intended, it is doubtful that this poem (unlike the one that follows) can be understood without reference to experiences the poet was apparently trying to objectify by the use of a mythic hero. At the time of its publication, Lewis was 53 years old. During his own second quarter of a century, he was converted to Roman Catholicism, and entered politics as one of the founders of Plaid Cymru, the Welsh Nationalist Party, and its president from 1926 to 1939. In 1936, together with two other party members, he committed a symbolic act of arson at Penyberth to protest the English government's insistence on basing an RAF bombing school on the Llŷn peninsula despite strong Welsh opposition, and was imprisoned for nine months in Wormwood Scrubs. After his release, the University College of Swansea refused to reinstate him as lecturer, and he experienced years of financial hardship, supporting his family by tenant-farming as well as journalism and teaching. He was Plaid Cymru's parliamentary candidate for the University of Wales constituency in 1943, losing in a bitter election to W. J. Gruffydd, a former ally.

Line 11 echoes Saint Matthew's Gospel, v, 25–6.

30 ARIANRHOD'S FORTRESS *Caer Arianrhod,* 1947
The Welsh name for the Milky Way.

Owain Glyndŵr, who claimed descent from the rulers of Powys and Gwynedd, led a Welsh rising against English rule and briefly succeeded in establishing himself as Prince of Wales during the first decade of the fifteenth century. The time and place of his death after his final defeat remain a mystery. There is a legend that the Abbot of Valle Crucis met Owain early one morning on the mountain of Berwyn; to Owain's comment that he had risen early, the Abbot replied that it was Owain who had risen early, a hundred years before his time, and Owain disappeared.

31 ELEGY FOR SIR JOHN EDWARD LLOYD *Marwnad Syr John Edward Lloyd*, 1948
J. E. Lloyd was professor of history at the University College of North Wales, Bangor, and author of *A History of Wales* and *Owen Glendower*. Saunders Lewis employs for the elegy the framework of medieval dream-vision poetry, alluding to Aeneas' journey to the underworld in Vergil's *Aeneid*, Book VI, at the beginning of the poem, and to Dante's *Inferno*, in which Vergil was the guide, at the end.

The third stanza refers to the prehistoric Celtic settlements in North Wales; the fourth to the Roman conquest of the region in the first century AD under Agricola, with allusions to the prophecy of Roman imperial rule Vergil had presented as made to Aeneas. The fifth stanza refers to the Christian missionaries of the sixth century; the sixth to the concept of a Holy Roman Empire, a united Christendom.

Cunedda was the fifth-century founder of a dynasty of Welsh rulers – medieval poets often use the term 'Cunedda's heirs' for the Welsh.

In the eighth stanza the warlord is Gruffudd ap Cynan, who died, old and blind, in 1137, attended by the Bishop of Bangor and other ecclesiastics. His struggles to gain control of north Wales in a period of Scandinavian raids and Norman invasions are the basis for allusions in the stanza – Hu Fras, Earl of Chester, temporarily imprisoned Gruffudd; at Bron yr Erw, Gruffudd suffered a severe defeat in battle; he was sheltered for a time in a cave in the district of Ardudwy.

The ninth stanza refers initially to the reign of Llywelyn the Great in the early thirteenth century, and particularly to the imprisonment of his wife Siwan and the public hanging of her lover, William de Braose. Although Llywelyn and Siwan were reconciled, she was buried as she had insisted apart from her husband; her body was taken by ship from Aberconwy to Beaumaris. The last lines in the stanza refer to the killing of

Llywelyn ap Gruffudd, who had proclaimed himself Prince of Wales, by English troops in 1282, and the execution of his brother Dafydd at Shrewsbury the following year, events which marked the end of Welsh independence.

For the references in the tenth stanza, see the earlier note on 'Arianrhod's Fortress'. The final stanza refers to the legendary prophecy of the Old Man of Pencader to King Henry II, that the Welsh would be conquered but their language would endure.

34   ELEGY FOR THOMAS GWYNN JONES *Marwnad Thomas Gwynn Jones, 1956*
Professor Gruffydd notes that the poem was dated 1950 when published in *Siwan a Cherddi Eraill,* but that he has thus far been unable to locate the periodical in which presumably it first appeared. For information on the subject of the elegy, see the earlier note on 'T. Gwynn Jones'.

Madog, etc.: references to T. Gwynn Jones's major poems dealing with Celtic legends.

councils' bungles: local councils in Wales have frequently failed to take measures supporting the Welsh language.

mongrel university: the colleges that comprise the University of Wales have all been, since their nineteenth-century beginnings, English-language institutions. T. Gwynn Jones was professor of Welsh literature at the University College of Wales, Aberystwyth, from 1919 to 1937.

Manion: 'Trifles' (1932), a collection of the poet's shorter works including translations from German, Irish, Italian, and Latin.

Cerddi: 'Poems'.

Anatiomaros: patriarchal teacher who in the poem named after him relates their ancestral history to a tribe living in 'Gwernyfed'. After a ceremony of rekindling divine fire on the hearths and purifying the tribe, Anatiamaros is found dead beside the altar at dawn, and his body is placed on a magnificent barge which floats downriver to the sea.

35   ASCENSION THURSDAY *Difiau Dyrchafael, 1950*
The feast-day celebrating the risen Jesus' ascension into heaven occurs forty days after Easter Sunday.

36   JUNE MOON *Lleuad Mehefin, 1950*

37 LAVERNOCK *Lavernock*, 1953
Lavernock is a promontory extending into the Bristol Channel, some two miles south of Saunders Lewis's home in Penarth.

38 OLD MAN *Hen Ŵr*, 1953

39 JOTTINGS – AUGUST 1953 *Nodiadau Mis Awst, 1953*

40 CAROL *Rhosyn Duw*, 1958
Saunders Lewis composed this Christmas carol to be set to music by Grace Williams, who composed a corresponding English version entitled 'The Flower of Bethlehem', published by Oxford University Press in 1958. I have not attempted to make my translation conform to this or any other musical setting.
    The first stanza refers to Jesus' descent through David and Jesse from Adam, and to the legend that the wood of the Cross grew from a seed in Adam's mouth.
    Sibyl: a reference to the prophetess of Cumae and Vergil's fourth eclogue, which in medieval times was interpreted as a prophecy of the birth of Christ.
    Eia Jesu : a greeting in Latin – 'Hail, Jesus'.

41 RETURN *Dychwelyd*, 1970

42 MAY IN THE GARDEN *Mai yn yr Ardd*, 1970

43 ET HOMO FACTUS EST. CRUCIFIXUS . . .1972
The title, translated as the first line of the poem, is from the Nicene Creed, which is recited as part of the liturgy of the Mass.
    a son is born: the prophecy of Isaiah, ix, 1–7, is read during the Midnight Mass for Christmas.
    Caiaphas: the Jewish high priest, said in Saint John's Gospel (xviii, 14) to have advised that it would be good if one man died for the people.
    Teiresias: the blind prophet in the ancient Greek story of Oedipus.

44 CHANCE CHILD *Plentyn Siawns*, 1972
    Marx: Karl Marx (1818–83), founder of Communism, believed a perfect, stateless, classless society would develop out of class struggle.

Teilhard de Chardin: Pierre Teilhard de Chardin (1881–1955), a Jesuit priest, scientist, and theologian, attempted to reconcile the theory of evolution with Christian doctrine by claiming that the human race was providentially evolving toward an 'Omega Point' of perfection.

45 MAY 1972. *Mai 1972,* 1972
Tutankhamûn: the ancient Egyptian pharaoh whose magnificent tomb was discovered in 1922.

46 PRAYER AT THE END   *Gweddi'r Terfyn,* 1973
The title, which has been rendered by others as 'The Final Prayer' and 'Terminal Prayer', resists English translation. *Terfyn* means 'limit', 'boundary', 'end' – in this case, not only death but the border-line between life and death, time and eternity, the finite and the infinite. And the prayer is not simply at the end but of the end – dying as in itself an act of praying.

The poem provoked a good deal of public discussion when first published, causing Saunders Lewis to note in Y *Tyst* (1974) his drawing upon those medieval mystical theologians who stress the inadequacy of human intellect, imagination, and language to comprehend or express the reality of God. A. M. Allchin has commented on the poem in the epilogue to his *Praise Above All* (University of Wales Press, 1991) as an example of 'the way of negation'.

47 A WORD TO THE WELSH   *Gair at y Cymry,* 1980
During the campaign to secure a Welsh-language television channel, the Reverend Professor Pennar Davies, Dr Meredydd Evans, and Ned Thomas, editor of *Planet,* switched off a television transmitter and were heavily fined. These are the 'three' referred to in the final line.
the Conquest: the Conquest of Wales is dated from the killing of Llywelyn ap Gruffudd, 'our last prince', in 1282.
the Union: Henry Tudor, of Welsh descent, achieved the English crown with considerable Welsh support in 1485. Under his son, Henry VIII, the Act of Union in 1536 annexed Wales politically to England, specifying English as the only language permitted for law and administration.
summa iniuria: the greatest harm.